THE PUBLIC RECORD OFFICE
MUSEUM
GUIDE

Opening hours

Monday, Wednesday, Friday: 9am – 5pm
Tuesday: 10am – 7pm
Thursday: 9am – 7pm
Saturday: 9.30am – 5pm

Last admissions 15 minutes before closing. Closed on public-holiday weekends. Admission is free. There is a shop, self-service restaurant and cyber-café on site.

For more information, contact:

Interpretation,
Public Record Office,
Richmond, Surrey TW9 4DU
tel: 020 8392 5202/5323
fax: 020 8392 5345
email: events@pro.gov.uk

You can visit the exhibition online at:
http://www.pro.gov.uk/virtualmuseum

There is a history in
all men's lives

Introduction

William Shakespeare

The Education and Visitor Centre is the Public Record Office's new museum. It showcases some of the most famous documents from the past 1,000 years, many of which have never before been on public display.

Domesday Book, Shakespeare's will, the logbook of HMS *Bounty*, a telegram from the *Titanic* and the signed confessions of Guy Fawkes all come together in this unique display of historic treasures. Visitors can explore everything from Famous Names to Crime and Punishment, and from War and Diplomacy to Kings and Queens. They can discover surprising facts about famous people, and the extraordinary feats of ordinary people. The centrepiece of the exhibition is the Treasury, which houses a cluster of our most priceless exhibits – including Britain's oldest public record.

The museum's exhibition is permanent, but the items on display are rotated regularly in order to conserve them for future generations. This also enables visitors to glimpse a greater range of documents from the rich and diverse collections of the Public Record Office.

The History of Record Keeping

For what is the worth of human life, unless it is woven into the life of our ancestors by the records of history?

Marcus Tullius Cicero

Early medieval kings regarded their records as akin to treasure, to be packed in great chests and transported in the royal baggage train. From the 12th century the royal headquarters settled down at London and Westminster; and from then until Queen Victoria's reign (1837–1901) the main State record offices were at Westminster Palace and Westminster Abbey (spreading out to Whitehall Palace from the 17th century), the Tower of London and the Rolls Estate, Chancery Lane.

It was at the latter site that the Public Record Office, founded in 1838, was built between 1852 and 1900. A contemporary described it as the 'strongbox of the Empire' and its design broke new ground in providing a secure, fireproof environment for the records. The Chancery Lane site also housed the first Public Record Office museum, which opened in 1902.

No less innovative in its time was the new building at Kew, West London, opened in 1977 to meet the needs of an ever expanding collection. Today it houses the vast bulk of the national archives of England, Wales and the United Kingdom – 100 shelf miles spanning 1,000 years of history.

Valor Ecclesiasticus, 1535
The Valor Ecclesiasticus (Latin for 'Church Valuation') was in effect Henry VIII's 'Domesday Book' for the Church. It told Henry VIII how much church wealth lay at his disposal in England and Wales after he had effectively appointed himself Head of the English Church. The dissolution of more than 800 monasteries began the following year.

E 344/22

The Treasury

History, with all her volumes vast....

Lord Byron

Great Domesday, 1086–90
Domesday Book is the earliest surviving public record. Based on a nation-wide survey of 1085–6 and drawn up on the orders of King William I, it describes in detail the landholdings and resources of England in the late 11th century. The native English gave it the nickname 'Domesday' Book after God's final Day of Judgement, when every soul would be assessed and against which there could be no appeal. Its official custodians, now the Public Record Office, have used this title since the 1170s.

E 31/2

Right: part of a typical entry in Great Domesday

Little Domesday, 1086
Little Domesday seems to represent the earliest stages of writing up the survey, and was perhaps a model on which Great Domesday was based. The work of several clerks, it was neatly but hurriedly compiled. 'Little' refers to its physical size, not the content. Indeed, it is more detailed than Great Domesday and less formally written.

E31/1

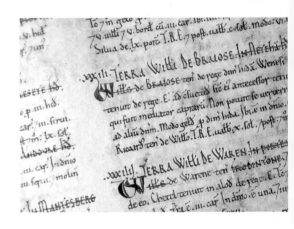

Magna Carta, 1225

Magna Carta (Latin for 'Great Charter') was issued by King John in 1215. It was essentially a peace agreement to prevent the most powerful men in the country from rebelling. As time went by, people gave greater importance to it, particularly the clauses that defined the rights of the subject against the king. Magna Carta was reissued three times under John's son, Henry III. The document shown here is the final, definitive form of the charter that entered the statute books as the first and most fundamental assertion of English rights.

DL 10/71

The most precious items of the collection are housed in the secure 'Treasury' area within the exhibition. It is here that Britain's oldest public record and the greatest treasure of the Public Record Office can be found: Domesday Book, commissioned by William the Conqueror in 1086 to provide a detailed survey of England. To minimize Domesday's exposure to light, its pages are carefully turned at regular intervals by conservators. The same is true for Valor Ecclesiasticus, Henry VIII's great survey of church wealth, which was completed in 1535. Some items, such as Magna Carta, are too fragile for permanent display and therefore need to be replaced by facsimiles. But it is not just documents that are on display in the Treasury. Among the most striking items are the solid gold seals of Henry VIII and his great rival, Francis I of France. Ironically, while these seals were made for a treaty of 'perpetual peace', they reflected the fierce rivalry between the two monarchs as each strove to produce the most magnificent seal.

Gold seals of Francis I and Henry VIII, 1527

Goldsmiths in England and France vied to create the most magnificent solid-gold seals for the Anglo-French Treaty of 1527. The seal (pictured above) produced for the French King, Francis I, shows him seated on a throne supported by lions and attended by angels.

Henry VIII's seal shows the king seated on a canopied throne and was probably designed by the famous artist Hans Holbein. The so-called 'perpetual peace' between the rival monarchs lasted only a few months.

PRO 30/26/82/1 and PRO 30/26/65

Queen Elizabeth II at the Public Record Office, 1978

In February 1978, HM Queen Elizabeth II visited the new Public Record Office site in Kew. The Kew building was significantly extended in 1995 to accommodate records from the PRO's central London site, in Chancery Lane, which was closed in 1997.

PRO 62/7

Kings and Queens

Robert Greene

Cartoon and photograph of Queen Victoria, 1878 and 1882

These contrasting images are of Britain's longest-reigning monarch, Queen Victoria (1837–1901). The photograph, taken in 1882, shows the Queen in characteristic mourning clothes. The colour sketch, by the famous cartoonist Bernhard Minchenberg, was made four years earlier, in 1878, when she was approaching 60.

COPY 1/57 f.388 and COPY 1/42 f.460

Queen Victoria's census return, 1851

Not even royalty could escape inclusion in the census returns, which began in 1801 and have continued every 10 years (with the exception of 1931 and 1941) ever since. This census return was taken at Buckingham Palace in 1851. Queen Victoria is entered simply as 'The Queen' under the heading Rank, Profession or Occupation. Prince Albert is listed as head of the household.

HO 107/1478

Second Great Seal of Elizabeth I, 1586

The second Great Seal of Elizabeth I, used from 1586 until her death in 1603, is loaded with symbolism. Heavenly rays above the Queen's head reflect her divinely sanctioned status, while the sceptre and orb that she holds are the traditional symbols of royal power. On the reverse side, Elizabeth is shown on horseback, riding across a field of flowering plants symbolizing hope, prosperity and femininity.

SC 13/N3

Edward VIII's letter of abdication, 1936

Edward VIII is the only British monarch to have abdicated. His decision, which was fiercely opposed by the Establishment, was prompted by his wish to marry Wallis Simpson, an American divorcee. The letter (left), signed and dated 10 December 1936, declares his 'irrevocable determination' to renounce the throne for himself and his descendants.

PC 11/1

The importance of the Crown has fluctuated over time. Medieval monarchs were surrounded by powerful nobles: strong kings extended their authority, while weak ones lost it. In the 17th century, royal power collapsed completely when Charles I was overthrown by Parliament and executed in 1649. After a brief period of government by Parliament alone (known as the Interregnum), followed by the Commonwealth, headed successively by Oliver Cromwell and his son Richard, the monarchy was restored in 1660 with the accession of Charles II. The Glorious Revolution of 1688, against James II, ensured that in future the monarch would always be constrained by partnership with Parliament.

The records trace the ebb and flow of royal power through the centuries. From the much maligned King Richard III to England's 'Gloriana' (Queen Elizabeth I), they give a fascinating – and often unexpected – insight into the private and public personas of Britain's ruling dynasties.

Letter from Richard III, 1483

Letter to the Lord Chancellor, the Bishop of Lincoln, dated 12 October 1483. Richard orders the Chancellor to send the Great Seal and officers of the Chancery, since he could not come in person by reason of his 'infirmities and diseases'. In the postscript he refers to the Duke of Buckingham as the 'most untrewe creature lyvyng'. The Duke rebelled against the King six days later and was beheaded.

C 81/1392 no.6

Swan marks, 1497–1515

Painted roll showing the distinguishing marks incised upon the bills of swans in Tudor Lincolnshire and Cambridgeshire. The swan has always been regarded as a 'bird royal' which no subject may own without a licence from the Crown. A 'swan-upping' takes place on the Thames every summer to mark the cygnets belonging to the Crown and to the Companies of Vintners and Dyers, who alone may keep swans on that river.

E 163/16/8

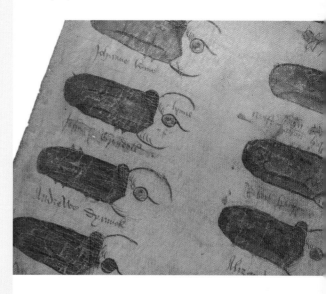

Letter from Charles Dickens, 1862
Letter from Charles Dickens to Lord Palmerston, dated at Gadshill Place on 13 August 1862. It concerns a memorial presented some months previously on behalf of his sister, Mrs Austin, widow of a civil engineer in the Local Government Act Office. Dickens bought Gadshill Place in March 1856 and lived there from 1860 until his death in 1870.

T 1/6486B/9043

Famous Names

And though her body die, her fame survives

John Milton

Robin Hood's wage account, 1324
'Robyn Hod' is listed as a porter of the King's Chamber in this wage account of 1324, when he was retired from service because he could no longer work. His retirement gift amounted to 20 days' wages. This could have been the legendary outlaw, although there are several other references to men named Robin Hood within the public records, the earliest dating from 1226.

E 101/380/4

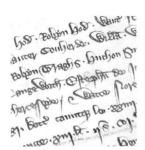

Lord Baden-Powell, 1911
Photograph of Lord Baden-Powell (front row, third from right) with a group of scoutmasters in Wales. The scouts in the background are spinning their hats on sticks. Baden-Powell founded the Boy Scout movement in 1908 and co-founded the Girl Guide movement in 1910.

COPY 1/558

Jane Austen's will, 1817
Jane Austen's will, written at her home in Chawton, Hampshire, on 27 April 1817, left everything to her beloved sister Cassandra, subject to payment of the funeral expenses and two legacies. Her total assets were valued at £800. She died in July of that year.
PROB 1/78

Florence Nightingale's birth registration, 1820
Florence Nightingale, who laid the basis of the modern nursing profession, became known as 'the Lady with the Lamp' because she carried an oil lamp round the hospital wards at night during the Crimean War.
RG 5/83 no.4058

Many famous names are scattered among the public records: from playwrights and explorers to politicians and pop stars. William Shakespeare, Robin Hood, Karl Marx, Florence Nightingale, Mahatma Gandhi, Harry Houdini, Charlie Chaplin, Sir Winston Churchill and Sir Elton John are all recorded in one way or another. They feature in the records for much the same reasons as anyone else. They are taxed or appear in the law courts, they are born, marry or die, they leave wills and sometimes letters. Others are here because of work done for the State – as soldiers, sailors or diplomats – and their reports and papers become part of the records. By reducing such renowned figures to the status of mere citizens, the records help to draw back the mask of fame and reveal the person beneath.

Shakespeare's will, 1616
William Shakespeare's will, dated 25 March 1616, shows that he was clearly a man of some means by the time of his death. He left the bulk of his estate to his elder daughter, Susannah Hall, but famously gave his wife, Anne Hathaway, nothing more than his 'second-best bed'.

Shakespeare's signature at the end of the will is one of only three known examples of the playwright's handwriting. He died a month later, on his birthday, 23 April, after catching a fever at a 'merry party' thrown by Ben Jonson, and was buried in the chancel of Stratford-upon-Avon church two days later.
PROB 1/4

Elton John's deed poll, 1972
Previously called Reginald Kenneth Dwight, the musician 'renounced, relinquished and abandoned' his former name on 6 January 1972. The deed poll shows that he chose 'Hercules' as his middle name.
J 18/458

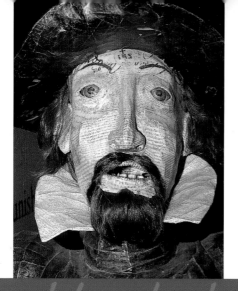

Confessions of Guy Fawkes, November 1605

Guy Fawkes signed two confessions – one after torture and another eight days later. The contrast between the two is remarkable. The one signed after torture is written in a frail and spidery hand, and Fawkes could only manage to write his first name, 'Guido'. The second is much bolder and the full name, 'Guido Fawkes', can be clearly read. Fawkes was subsequently tried before a special commission and executed on 31 January 1606.

SP 14/216

Papier-mâché sculpture of Guy Fawkes in the PRO museum

the bloody book of law
Crime and Punishment
You shall yourself read in the bitter letter

William Shakespeare

Dick Turpin and Black Bess, 1739

'Indictment of John Palmer, alias Richard Turpin, late of the castle of York, labourer, for stealing a black mare worth three pounds, and a filly foal worth twenty shillings, from Thomas Creasey at Welton, Yorkshire, on 1 March 1739.' The mare referred to was Turpin's trusty steed, Black Bess. Turpin pleaded not guilty to the charge, but was found guilty and hanged at York.

ASSI 44/54

Trial record of Charles I, 1649

Formal record of the proceedings of the High Court of Justice, convened for the trial of Charles I. The King refused to accept the legality of the court and would not answer the numerous charges made against him. He was found guilty and executed on the balcony of the Banqueting House, Whitehall, on 30 January 1649.

SP 16/517

Photographs of Victorian prisoners from Oxford Gaol, 1870–81

This album shows photographs of prisoners in Oxford Gaol. The ages of the prisoners vary widely. William James, aged 78, was sentenced to two months' imprisonment for stealing a watch; the child convict, Julia Ann Crumpling, aged 7 (pictured here), served seven days' hard labour for stealing a perambulator.

PCOM 2/352

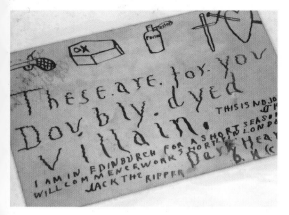

'Jack the Ripper' postcard, September/October 1888

The murders committed by 'Jack the Ripper' remain one of the greatest unsolved mysteries in British criminal history. Between August and November 1888, six prostitutes were found murdered within an area of London's East End one mile square. Despite extensive police investigations, the killer was never caught. Scotland Yard received a flood of letters from hoaxers claiming to be the Ripper. The postcard shown here bears various gruesome illustrations, and ends 'I am in Edinburgh for a short season. Will commence work shortly in London. Jack the Ripper.'

MEPO 3/142

One of the legacies of Magna Carta was the English attachment to trial by jury: 'No free man shall be imprisoned, except by the lawful judgement of his peers.' Through the ages, this 'lawful judgement' has taken the form of whipping, branding, transportation and even death. The varying severity of English common law is well documented by the public records. The crime of stealing a perambulator earned Julia Ann Crumpling, aged 7, a week's hard labour in 1870, while convicted traitors such as Guy Fawkes and Sir Thomas More suffered a much harsher fate. In the statements of criminals and witnesses, we hear the voices of our forebears and something of their struggle to survive.

The imprisonment of Sir Thomas More, 1534–5

Sir Thomas More was committed to the Tower in April 1534 on a charge of treason for refusing to acknowledge Henry VIII as head of the new Church of England. Both he and his servants were interrogated repeatedly by Henry's Commissioners, as described by the document shown here. More was found guilty and executed on Tower Hill on 6 July 1535. His last words asserted that he 'died his [the King's] good servant, but God's first'.

SP 1/93 f.52

Cato Street Conspirators' spikes, 1820

In 1820 a group of political reformists conspired to assassinate members of the Cabinet and display their heads on spikes, two of which are shown here. But a Government spy had infiltrated the group, and on the night of the attempted assassination the conspirators were arrested and taken to gaol as they were preparing to leave a room in Cato Street. Four of the group were executed for high treason and another five were transported. The spikes were used as evidence at their trial.

TS 11/208

Death mask of Dr John Yonge, 1516

Dr John Yonge enjoyed a distinguished career as custodian of public records. He was Master of the Rolls from 1508 until his death in 1516, and was also frequently employed by Henry VII and Henry VIII on important diplomatic missions. Other versions of Yonge's death mask can be found in Westminster Abbey and the National Portrait Gallery.

SC 16/29

Birth, Marriage and Death

For we are the people of England That never have spoken yet

GK Chesterton

Effects of Mary Smith, 1811

Mary Smith was described as a 'lunatic' and once lived at Christ's Hospital in London. Her effects were entered into the court of Chancery as exhibits some time after her death. They include a medallion commemorating the King of Prussia's victory at the Battle of Rosbach in 1757, three miniatures in individual cases, a silver box, and a gold watch.

C 114/190

Miniature Gothic font, c. 1840

This miniature Wedgwood porcelain font is in the Gothic style and has been dated to about 1840. It was used for baptisms in the Rolls Chapel at the PRO's former site in Chancery Lane. The Rolls Chapel was used for the celebration of divine service from 1232 until 1895.

SC 16/33

Letter from Catherine Howard to Thomas Culpepper, 1541

Letter from Catherine Howard, fifth wife of Henry VIII, to her lover, Thomas Culpepper. Catherine was much younger than the ageing king and rumours soon began to circulate of her affair with Culpepper, a great favourite at court. This affectionate letter was seized by Henry's men and helped seal her doom. She was executed in February 1542.

SP 1/167 f.14

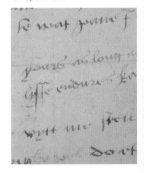

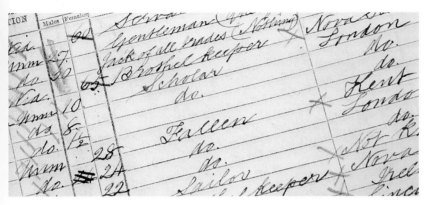

Census return for Albert Square, 1871
True to the television series, the Albert Square in this census return is also in the East End of London, at St Paul's, Shadwell. Most of the women are described as 'Fallen', while the men are listed as 'Sailors'. This is a fair indication that most of the houses within the square were used as brothels.

RG 10/544 f.117

For much of history, the State has been concerned with recording details about property rather than individuals. Evidence from legal trials – such as the possessions of Mary Smith or a love letter from Catherine Howard – occasionally provides insights into both famous and ordinary lives. But it was not until the early 19th century that formal means for recording details of citizens' lives were introduced. Campaigns for the rights of all subjects and concerns about public health led to the creation of two sets of records of great value to family historians today. Civil registration of the birth, marriage and death of all inhabitants of England and Wales began in 1837. Meanwhile, the first census was commissioned in 1801 and has been carried out every 10 years, with the exception of 1941. It records the name, address, occupation and place and date of birth of every person in England and Wales, and is the most heavily used record in the Public Record Office.

Pit girls, 1893
These 'pit brow' girls were photographed in 1893, just before they started work. Above them the coal wagon announces who these little workers belong to: W & J Turner, Wigan Junction Colliery, Wigan. The photograph gives workers and wagon equal status – both have a job to do.

COPY 1/412 f.2

List of drowned passengers on RMS *Titanic*, April 1912
RMS *Titanic* sank in the early hours of 15 April 1912 after colliding with an iceberg in the Atlantic Ocean. Of the 2,228 passengers and members of the crew on board, only 705 survived. The detail shown here is from the official report listing the names of passengers who perished.

BT 100/260 f.132

Waterloo campaign medal, 1815
This medal was awarded to driver William Gallas of the King's German Artillery. It was enclosed in his discharge papers, dated 24 February 1816, and was found among the archives of the British Legation in Frankfurt.

FO 208/89

War and Diplomacy

They shall grow not old, as we that are left grow old

Laurence Binyon

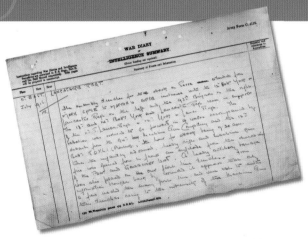

The Battle of the Somme, 1 July 1916
Unit War Diary entry for the 11th (Service) Battalion of the East Lancashire Regiment – the 'Accrington Pals' – on the first day of the Battle of the Somme. Intended to be the 'big push', the Somme campaign instead saw appalling loss of life.

Of the Accrington Pals, 234 died and at least 360 were wounded. One of the battalion, Lance Corporal Marshall, observed: 'I need hardly say what it was like – but if hell is like a battlefield, then God help the sinner.'

WO 95/2366

D-Day, 1944
Order of the day and message to the troops issued by the Allied Supreme Commander, General Eisenhower, dated 6 June 1944. D-Day was the code name for Operation 'Overlord', the Allies' great assault on the Germans in Western Europe.

WO 219/5120

The 'Dam Busters', 1943
Page from the Operations Record Book of 617 Squadron, which carried out the raid on the German dams in the Ruhr on the night of 16/17 May 1943, using the new 'bouncing bombs'. Thirty-three decorations were awarded to the aircrew who took part in the raids, including the V.C. for Wing Commander Guy Gibson, who led 617 Squadron.

AIR 27/839

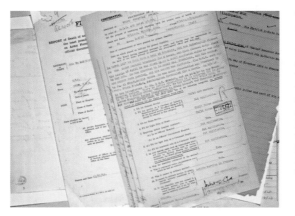

Wilfred Owen's service record
Extracts from the service record of the First World War soldier and poet Wilfred Owen. The medical officer describes the injuries Owen sustained while serving in France in the spring of 1917, and adds that he was 'of a highly strung temperament'. Owen was killed in action on 4 November 1918, just one week before the end of the war.

WO 138/74

T he people of these islands have experienced numerous wars, at home and abroad, since William the Conqueror's invasion in 1066. The records preserved in the Public Record Office describe the build-up to and consequences of these wars, as well as defence policies, diplomatic negotiations and, above all, the people – both military and civil – who were affected by war. The signing-on papers of those serving in the First World War are the descendants of the indentures of medieval soldiers who fought at Agincourt. From the late 18th century, service records tell us what individual servicemen looked like; and military operations are described in maps and dispatches from commanders in the field such as Wellington, Nelson and Montgomery. Individual acts of bravery at Waterloo and the Somme may be set alongside notorious atrocities such as Hitler's persecution of the Jews. Together, the records chart the shifting boundaries of territories and nations, within the British Isles and across the world.

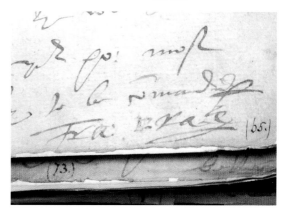

Hitler's face on a matchbox, c. 1940–5
A matchbox showing a snake in the image of Adolf Hitler, from a series of American propaganda materials. All the leading combatants in the Second World War used propaganda. With the establishment of the Political Warfare Executive in August 1941, British propaganda began in earnest. Its tools included the ordinary news media, leaflets and graffiti.

EXT 5/10

Sir Francis Drake and the Armada, 1588
Sir Francis Drake, Vice-Admiral of the English fleet, wrote this letter to Sir Francis Walsingham, Elizabeth I's Secretary, after the Battle of Gravelines on 29 July 1588, which proved to be the decisive engagement of the 10-day running fight with the Spanish Armada. 'This dayes servis', he observed, 'hathe much apald the enemey and no doubt but incoraged our armey.'

SP 12/213 no.65

Victorian fashion cutouts, 1885

These paper cutouts were produced in 1885. The clothes are designed to be cut out and fixed to the figures with tabs. They give an interesting insight into the fashions of the Victorian era, both for adults and children, and include all kinds of clothing – from petticoats and bustles to skirts and smocks.

COPY 1/67

Invention, Fashion and Design

RW Emerson

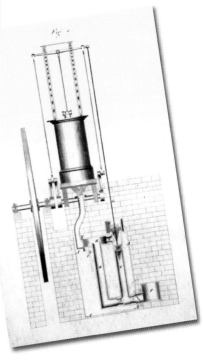

Stephenson's *Rocket*, 1822

In 1822 George Stephenson won a competition to design an engine to pull the trains on the proposed Manchester to Liverpool railway with his steam engine, the *Rocket*. Within the public records is the enrolled specification for his design (right), as well as a photograph of a replica *Rocket* (above).

COPY 1/376

Crystal Palace wallpaper design, 1851
Wallpaper design from 1851 featuring the Great Exhibition buildings in Hyde Park, later re-erected at Crystal Palace. From 1839, designs for manufactured goods such as fabrics, pottery and metalwork were protected by the registration of designs. Registered copies of the protected designs up to 1964 are now held at the Public Record Office.

BT 43/88 no.78974

Austin radio car, 1931
In 1931, as part of an experiment to explore signals and reception, a redesigned Austin car was fitted with special radio equipment. The finished product is shown here.

AVIA 23/542

The public records are a wonderful source for the history of design and technology. From the late 16th century, inventors and designers could defend their work from exploitation by securing a grant of letters patent. Plans and drawings could also be enrolled for legal protection from 1730, and in the 19th century designs were registered for copyright purposes. Samples of fabrics, clothing and wallpaper, plus drawings and photographs, give a glimpse of the tastes and fashions of our forebears. Wallpaper designs showing scenes from the Great Exhibition sit alongside paper cutouts of Victorian clothes. Revolutions in transport and communication are also well documented. There are Stephenson's plans for the *Rocket* in 1822, a telegram sent from the *Titanic* and photographs of a radio-operated car from the 1930s. Such documents remind us of the legacy left by some of the greatest British inventors and designers.

SOS telegram sent from RMS *Titanic*, 14-15 April 1912
Original copy of the telegram sent by wireless operator Jack Phillips (above) as the *Titanic* (code name MGY) started to sink after being hit by an iceberg on her maiden voyage across the *Atlantic*. The telegram was received by the Russian steamer SS *Birma* and tersely states: 'WE ARE SINKING FAST PASSENGERS BEING PUT INTO BOATS'.

MT 9/920C

Caxton, printed indulgence, 1476
This is the earliest document known to have been printed in England. It is a Latin 'indulgence' – a pardon issued by the Church – given by John, Abbot of Abingdon, to Henry Lanley of London and Katherine his wife. The indulgence was printed on 13 December 1476 by William Caxton, who introduced printing to England.

E 135/6/56

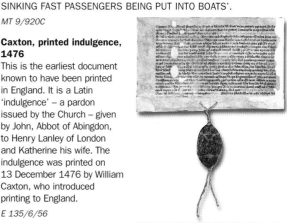

Gold coins, 1780s

These coins could be described as pirates' booty. They were found in the Admiralty Prize Court Miscellany, and the official description of the document 'Intercepted mails and papers Dutch 1780–7' gives little idea of the unexpected treasure inside. The High Court of Admiralty issued licences to allow private individuals to undertake such 'piracy' against enemy trading vessels in time of war.

HCA 65/6

Treaty of Amity signed by George Washington, 1794

The loss of the American colonies and the events of the American War of Independence (1775–83) had severely shaken Britain's confidence. However, trade with the newly independent United States of America soon began to grow. This trading relationship between Britain and her former colony was formalized in 1794 by the Treaty of Amity.

FO 94/2

Wider World

John Cabot's voyage of discovery, 1496

In March 1496, Henry VII issued these letters patent to John Cabot authorizing his voyage in search of unknown lands. Cabot was a Venetian who had settled in England. Having secured the King's support, he and his three sons set out in search of new lands, in return for which he shrewdly demanded a share of any profits.

C 76/178

Shoa Treaty, 16 November 1841

The occupation of Aden, in Arabia, by Britain in 1839 led to an attempt to open communications with Shoa, in Africa, on the other side of the Red Sea. The treaty was agreed at a time when the ancient Christian kingdom of Ethiopia had almost fallen apart into its separate provinces, of which Shoa was one, and rival emperors had become a regular feature.

FO 93/94/1

Map of New York, 1765

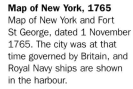

Map of New York and Fort St George, dated 1 November 1765. The city was at that time governed by Britain, and Royal Navy ships are shown in the harbour.

MPI 1/68

Ordinances of the Order of St Michael presented to Henry VIII, 1527

By 1527 English foreign policy had swung towards alliance with France. The symbol of this friendship was the admission of both Henry VIII and Francis I into each other's orders of chivalry. On 10 November 1527, at his palace in Greenwich, Henry received the Order of St Michael from a party of French ambassadors, who also presented him with this beautifully illuminated volume.

E36/276

T he sea has been our pathway from these small islands to the wider world. Before the 20th century, poor communications and perilous travel made the world a much larger place than it is today. Yet this did not deter explorers such as John Cabot and Captain Cook from embarking upon daring expeditions to seek new lands and fortunes. Nor did it deter the thousands of ordinary people who sought a new life beyond these shores. By the end of the 19th century, many people had the experience of emigration, forced or voluntary, somewhere in their family. The records set the experience of individuals in the context of Britain's contact with the wider world, which forms a shifting pattern of hostilities and alliances. Long and fruitful alliances like the Treaty of Amity with the USA are contrasted with short-lived and uneasy pacts such as Henry VIII's 'perpetual peace' with France. A more permanent link to the wider world was envisaged by William Tolliday, who in 1895 drew up a scheme for a tunnel under the English Channel. Almost a century later, a handshake through a hole deep under the Channel marked the realization of his dream.

Anglo-Spanish Treaty, 1605

When Philip III of Spain ratified the Treaty of London, at Valladolid in the late spring of 1605, he brought to an end almost two decades of warfare between Spain and England. It was common for treaty ratifications to depict the monarchs of each country involved. The embellishments on the copy presented to James I of England (shown here) included a portrait of the Spanish king, as well as the royal arms.

E 30/1705

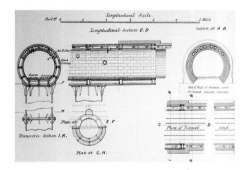

Channel Tunnel plans, 1875

Plans for a Channel Tunnel railway link between Calais and Dover, drawn up in 1875. The idea for a tunnel linking Britain to France dates back to the Napoleonic Wars, but the first serious moves were not made until the 1860s. In 1882 work started on a pilot tunnel from Folkestone, but was halted by the British government because of fears regarding national security.

MFQ 1/954

Indian independence
This photograph shows the Aga Khan with Mahatma Gandhi – the man who was above all the architect of Indian independence – at the Round Table Conference of 1931 in London. The conference helped pave the way for Indian independence, but it was not until 1947 that this was finally achieved.

ZPER 34/179 f.526

Illuminated Jubilee address in gilt cabinet, from the city of Adelaide, 1897
This beautiful gilt cabinet was presented to Queen Victoria by the city of Adelaide to mark her Diamond Jubilee, 22 June 1897. The day was proclaimed a holiday, and celebrations were staged across the British Empire.

PP 1/636

Britain, Empire and Commonwealth

The Empire on which the sun never set

Southern Rhodesia seal matrix, Elizabeth II
Matrix for the seal of Southern Rhodesia, with copper counterpart. Rhodesia, the region between Bechuanaland (now Botswana) and the Zambezi River, was named after Cecil Rhodes and administered by his British South Africa Company. It secured internationally recognized independence from Britaín, as Zimbabwe, in 1980.

DO 122/1–2

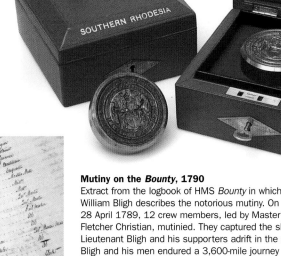

Mutiny on the *Bounty*, 1790
Extract from the logbook of HMS *Bounty* in which Lieutenant William Bligh describes the notorious mutiny. On the morning of 28 April 1789, 12 crew members, led by Master's Mate Fletcher Christian, mutinied. They captured the ship and set Lieutenant Bligh and his supporters adrift in the ship's launch. Bligh and his men endured a 3,600-mile journey to Timor in this open boat, and arrived back in Britain as heroes. Some of the mutineers were later captured in Tahiti and brought back to stand trial. Other members of the crew decided not to return to their homeland and founded a British colony on Pitcairn Island.

ADM 55/151

TOGETHER

Call-up poster for the Empire, Second World War
At the outbreak of the Second World War, Britain did not stand alone. The dominions of her Empire and Commonwealth comprised about one quarter of the world's land and population. This call-up poster, produced by the Ministry of Information, was used to encourage the men of the Empire to join the fighting services.
INF 2/3

When Queen Victoria celebrated her Diamond Jubilee in 1897, she ruled an Empire on which the sun literally never set. Britain had colonies in every continent, which together comprised more than a quarter of the world's land surface. By the mid 20th century, the picture was quite different. Many parts of the Empire had or were gaining their independence. India, the 'Jewel in the Crown', became independent in 1947. Most, but not all, ex-colonies joined together in the Commonwealth, a new conception built on 'friendship, loyalty and the desire for freedom'.

The public records chronicle the development of the British Empire, from its beginnings in the late 16th century to its demise in the 20th. They also chart the movement of people between Britain and her Empire. Many Britons spent years living in the colonies, and some chose to settle there permanently. The traffic was in both directions, and Britain now has a vibrant mix of people and cultures from all parts of the world, living as citizens together.

Letter from James Cook to Philip Stephens, Secretary of the Admiralty, 1768
HMS *Endeavour's* voyage of 1768–71 aimed to assist the Royal Society in making astronomical observations from Tahiti. However, its greatest achievement was the survey of the previously unknown east coast of Australia. The letter shown here is from James Cook to Philip Stephens, Secretary of the Admiralty, asking for mathematical instruments and stationery for use on the forthcoming voyage.
ADM 1/1609

Passenger list for the SS *Empire Windrush*, 1948
Immediately after the Second World War many West Indians who had seen war service in the UK returned here in search of better career opportunities. On 22 June 1948, the SS *Empire Windrush* arrived at Tilbury docks carrying the first large consignment of immigrants (492 in all) from the Caribbean. A sculpture of one of the passengers, Lucilda Harris, can be seen in the PRO's museum.
BT 26/1237

Above: Illustration showing the shallop bearing Nelson's body from Greenwich to Whitehall on 8 January 1806, published by Ackermann's *Repository of Arts* (LC 2/40)

Front cover: PRO Virtual Museum montage by Harpal Sabharwal
(adapted for the cover by Blueprint Design Consultants, Kew Gardens)

Back cover: Seal of Francis I (PRO 30/26/82/1) and the indictment of John Palmer, alias Dick Turpin (ASSI 44/54)

Page 1: Display case in the PRO museum, containing Magna Carta, Domesday Book and Valor Ecclesiasticus, photograph © Hugh Alexander

Page 3: Tudor wallpaper (SC 16/53)

Page 5: Part of an entry in Great Domesday (E 31/2)

Page 5: The Public Record Office, Kew, photograph © Hugh Alexander

Page 10: Panel of portraits from the entrance to the PRO museum, produced for the PRO by the JANVS Group Ltd, York

Page 11: Portraits of Jane Austen (NPG 3630) and Sir Thomas More (NPG 4358) reproduced by courtesy of the National Portrait Gallery, London

Page 12: Sculpture of Guy Fawkes, photograph © Hugh Alexander

Page 13: Cato Street Conspirators' spikes, photograph © Hugh Alexander

Except as indicated above, all the images included in this book are from the Public Record Office Image Library

Public Record Office
Richmond
Surrey
TW9 4DU

© Tracy Borman 2001

ISBN 1 903365 14 7

British Library Cataloguing-in-Publication Data
A catalogue record for this book is available from the British Library

Designed by Blueprint Design Consultants, Kew Gardens
Printed by Apollo Printing Services Ltd, West Molesey